Group®
Loveland, Colorado

WHO IS Jesus?

A 4-week course to help senior highers come to know Jesus as friend, teacher and savior

by Dick Hardel

Group®

Who Is Jesus?
Copyright © 1991 Group Publishing, Inc.

Credits
Edited by Stephen Parolini
Cover designed by Jill Christopher and DeWain Stoll
Interior designed by Judy Bienick and Jan Aufdemberge
Illustrations by Raymond Medici

ISBN 1-55945-219-6

13 12 11 10 9 8   04 03 02 01 00
Printed in the United States of America.

Visit our Web site: www.grouppublishing.com

CONTENTS

WHO IS JESUS?

Behind Jesus' every parable and miracle lies the powerful question, "Who is Jesus?" It's a haunting question that echoes through the gospels: Who is this one who can calm the wind and the seas, heal the sick, cast out demons, forgive sins, teach with authority, love with honest compassion and communicate a word without speaking?

This same question perplexes teenagers today.

• • •

"Well, he *was* a great man . . . " began Ryan.

"Yeah, but he was God, too, wasn't he?" asked Tony.

"Not if you listen to my history teacher," said Cindy. "He believes Jesus was a great teacher . . . but that's it. The rest is a myth according to him."

"But, you don't agree, do you? I mean, if Jesus was just a man, how could he rise from the dead? What would that mean to your faith?"

• • •

What significance do the stories of Jesus have in the lives of your teenagers? A study by Search Institute on effective Christian

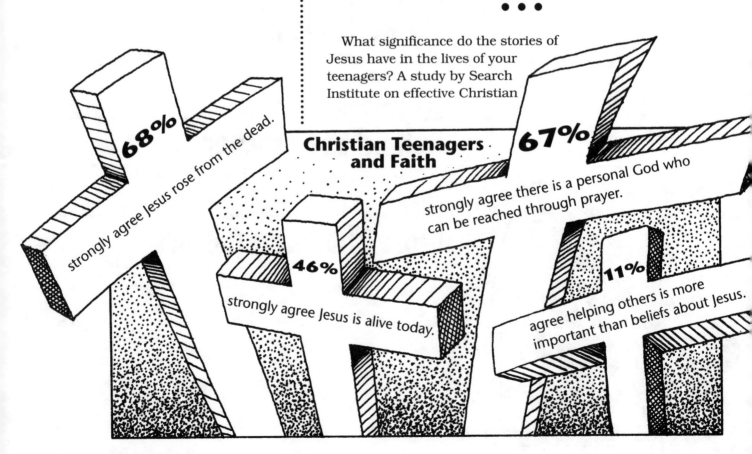

Christian Teenagers and Faith

68% strongly agree Jesus rose from the dead.

67% strongly agree there is a personal God who can be reached through prayer.

46% strongly agree Jesus is alive today.

11% agree helping others is more important than beliefs about Jesus.

education found that 64 percent of Christian teenagers in the United States have an underdeveloped faith.

Sunday school needs to teach teenagers more than stories about Jesus. The church's role is to help teenagers develop a solid understanding of who Jesus is—and develop a close relationship with him.

Each lesson in this course is full of powerful questions of faith and life. *Who Is Jesus?* will not only help kids explore the biblical accounts of Jesus' life, but will help teenagers answer the question, "Who is Jesus?" from their own faith perspective.

Use this course to help your teenagers get to know Jesus as human and divine, master teacher, friend and conqueror over death.

By the end of this course, your students will:
● struggle with the question, "Who is Jesus?";
● identify Jesus as their best friend;
● discover Jesus as master teacher;
● learn how Jesus has conquered death; and
● celebrate Jesus' presence.

COURSE OBJECTIVES

HOW TO USE THIS COURSE

ACTIVE LEARNING

Think back on an important lesson you've learned in life. Did you learn it from reading about it? from hearing about it? from something you experienced? Chances are the most important lessons you've learned came from something you've experienced. That's what active learning is—learning by doing. And active learning is a key element in Group's Active Bible Curriculum.

Active learning leads students in doing things that help them understand important principles, messages and ideas. It's a discovery process that helps kids internalize what they learn.

Each lesson section in Group's Active Bible Curriculum plays an important part in active learning:

The **Opener** involves kids in the topic in fun and unusual ways.

The **Action and Reflection** includes an experience designed to evoke specific feelings in the students. This section also processes those feelings through "How did you feel?" questions and applies the message to situations kids face.

The **Bible Application** actively connects the topic with the Bible. It helps kids see how the Bible is relevant to the situations they face.

The **Commitment** helps students internalize the Bible's message and commit to make changes in their lives.

The **Closing** funnels the lesson's message into a time of creative reflection and prayer.

When you put all the sections together, you get a lesson that's fun to teach. And kids get messages they'll remember.

BEFORE THE 4-WEEK SESSION

● Read the Introduction, the Course Objectives and This Course at a Glance.

● Decide how you'll publicize the course using the clip art on the Publicity Page (p. 9). Prepare fliers, newsletter articles and posters as needed.

● Look at the Bonus Ideas (p. 45) and decide which ones you'll use.

● Read the opening statements, Objectives and Bible Basis for the lesson. The Bible Basis shows how specific passages relate to senior highers today.

● Choose which Opener and Closing options to use. Each is appropriate for a different kind of group.

● Gather necessary supplies from This Lesson at a Glance.

● Read each section of the lesson. Adjust where necessary for your class size and meeting room.

BEFORE EACH LESSON

● The approximate minutes listed give you an idea of how long each activity will take. Each lesson is designed to take 35 to 60 minutes. Shorten or lengthen activities as needed to fit your group.

● If you see you're going to have extra time, do an activity or two from the "If You Still Have Time . . ." box or from the Bonus Ideas (p. 45).

● Dive into the activities with the kids. Don't be a spectator. The lesson will be more successful and rewarding to both you and your students.

● Though some kids may at first think certain activities are "silly," they'll enjoy them, and they'll remember the messages from these activities long after the lesson is over. As one Active Bible Curriculum user has said, "I can ask the kids questions about a lesson I did three weeks ago, and they actually remember what I taught!" And that's the whole idea of teaching . . . isn't it?

Have fun with the activities you lead. Remember, it was Jesus who encouraged us to become "like little children." Besides, how often do your kids get *permission* to express their childlike qualities?

HELPFUL HINTS

● The answers given after discussion questions are responses your students *might* give. They aren't the only answers or the "right" answers. If needed, use them to spark discussion. Kids won't always say what you wish they'd say. That's why some of the responses given are negative or controversial. If someone responds negatively, don't be shocked. Accept the person, and use the opportunity to explore other angles of the issue.

THIS COURSE AT A GLANCE

Before you dive into the lessons, familiarize yourself with each lesson aim. Then read the scripture passages.
- Study them as a background to the lessons.
- Use them as a basis for your personal devotions.
- Think about how they relate to kids' circumstances today.

LESSON 1: GOD AND MAN

Lesson Aim: To help senior highers see Jesus as both human and divine.

Bible Basis: Luke 24:36-49 and John 1:1-18.

LESSON 2: MY BEST FRIEND

Lesson Aim: To help senior highers see Jesus as a friend who desires to walk with them daily.

Bible Basis: John 15:9-17.

LESSON 3: BEHOLD THE TEACHER

Lesson Aim: To help senior highers see Jesus as the master teacher.

Bible Basis: Matthew 7:28-29 and Mark 4:1-2.

LESSON 4: MORE THAN CONQUERORS

Lesson Aim: To help senior highers understand the impact of Jesus' victory over death.

Bible Basis: John 20:19-31; Romans 6:1-14; and Romans 8:31-39.

PUBLICITY PAGE

G rab your senior highers' attention! Photocopy this page, and then cut out and paste the clip art of your choice in your church bulletin or newsletter to advertise this course on understanding Jesus. Or photocopy and use the ready-made flier as a bulletin insert. Permission to photocopy this clip art is granted for local church use.

Splash the clip art on posters, fliers or even postcards! Just add the vital details: the date and time the course begins and where you'll meet.

It's that simple.

A 4-week high school course on getting to know Jesus

Come to _____

On _____

At _____

Come discover a closer relationship with Jesus!

GOD AND MAN

I f asked the question, "Who is Jesus?" many teenagers wouldn't know how to respond. They might answer that Jesus was a good man—and nothing else. Or they might decide Jesus couldn't have been both human and divine.

Today's non-Christian beliefs portray Jesus in many different ways—ways that don't always match the Bible's portrayal of Jesus. By exploring the Bible's picture of Jesus as truly God and truly human, teenagers can learn to confidently answer the question, "Who is Jesus?"

To help senior highers see Jesus as both human and divine.

LESSON AIM

Students will:
- **explore the difference between observing people and becoming like them;**
- **discover the importance of God becoming human in Jesus;**
- **describe their faith; and**
- **learn how Jesus is present in the midst of their questions.**

OBJECTIVES

Look up the following scriptures. Then read the background paragraphs to see how the passages relate to your senior highers.

Luke 24:36-49 describes Jesus' appearance to the disciples and others following his Resurrection.

In this passage, Luke draws attention to Jesus' hands and feet and his hunger to establish that he is indeed a human being—not a ghost or spirit.

Just as the disciples saw Jesus as true man and true God, teenagers today can see Jesus for who he is. They can begin to understand how Jesus knows their feelings—since he was

BIBLE BASIS

LUKE 24:36-39
JOHN 1:1-18

once a human. And they can begin to understand how Jesus can lead them—since he is also God.

In **John 1:1-18**, the author describes God becoming human. As John describes the "Word" that was with God from the beginning of time, he is describing Jesus. This passage is significant because it helps us see a connection between our lives and our faith in Jesus Christ. John wants us to understand that the Word became flesh—that God became man.

When teenagers begin to explore who Jesus is, they may not fully understand Jesus' relationship with God. This passage points out that Jesus was with God from the beginning of time, that Jesus was and is God, and that Jesus was human. It's not an easy concept to understand, but teenagers can begin to grasp the big picture of who Jesus is through these verses.

THIS LESSON AT A GLANCE

Section	Minutes	What Students Will Do	Supplies
Opener (Option 1)	up to 5	**Line Up**—Line up on a continuum based on their responses to statements about Jesus.	Masking tape
(Option 2)		**Picture This**—List words describing who Jesus is.	Newsprint, markers, tape
Action and Reflection	15 to 20	**Stooping Down**—Talk about what it's like to be a child, then become like children.	3×5 cards, pencils, children's toys
Bible Application	15 to 20	**Making the Word Come Alive**—Discover how God becoming flesh helps us know him better.	Blindfolds, miscellaneous items, Bible
Commitment	5 to 10	**I Still Have Questions**—Explore who Jesus is, and commit to learn more about him.	Pencils, paper
Closing (Option 1)	up to 5	**Joyful Noise**—Listen to or sing a song together.	Tape player, music tape, songbooks (optional)
(Option 2)		**Just Like Me**—Mold clay to represent how they feel about Jesus and pray for each other.	Modeling clay

The Lesson

☐ OPTION 1: LINE UP

Use masking tape to draw a line down the middle of the floor. Say: **After I read a statement, stand along the line according to how you feel about the statement. This end** (point to one end of the line) **means you agree completely and the other end** (point to the other end of the line) **means you disagree completely.**

Read aloud each of the following statements. Allow time for kids to each find a spot to stand along the continuum.

- **Most of my friends think Jesus was a great man.**
- **Jesus is God.**
- **Jesus was a good teacher.**
- **Jesus walked the earth as a human.**
- **Jesus never really died.**
- **Jesus rose from the dead.**
- **Jesus is both human and divine.**
- **If someone asked me who Jesus is, I could confidently explain who he is.**
- **I'd like to know more about who Jesus is.**

Have kids sit down. Then ask:

- **What did you notice about the way people responded to these statements?** (We didn't always agree; people see Jesus differently.)
- **How did you feel as you decided how to respond?** (Unsure; confident.)
- **How is that like the way some people feel when they think about who Jesus is?** (Some people are unsure who Jesus is; some people are confident about who Jesus is.)

Say: **Each of us has a different perception of who Jesus is. And that's okay. But what can we learn about Jesus that will help us grow closer to him? Today we'll begin our course on** *Who Is Jesus?* **by discovering Jesus as truly God and truly human.**

☐ OPTION 2: PICTURE THIS

Draw two large picture frames on newsprint and tape them on opposite walls. Form two teams and give each team one marker. Have team members line up in the center of the room, each facing a different newsprint frame.

Say: **When I say "go," one person from each team must run up to his or her newsprint to write a one- or two-word response to the question, "Who is Jesus?" The response can be something you believe about Jesus or something someone else believes. Then team members must each run back to their team and hand the marker to the next** person in line. This person must then run up and follow the same instructions.

We'll continue, with one person from each team writing at a time, until I say stop. The object is to come up with a word-picture of Jesus.

Say "go" and allow two minutes for teams to compete. Then call time and have teams compare their "pictures" of Jesus.

Ask:

● **How did you feel as you tried to think of a description of Jesus?** (Confident; unsure; it was easy at first; I didn't know what to write.)

● **How is that like the way some people feel when they try to understand who Jesus is?** (They feel confused; they feel unsure.)

Say: **Each of us probably has a different picture of who Jesus is. We may see him as serious or happy. We may see him with long hair or short hair. We may see him as teacher or preacher. But however we see him, each picture of Jesus is incomplete unless we see him as both God and man. Today we'll focus on the picture of Jesus as truly God and truly human—and the questions that arise from that picture.**

ACTION AND REFLECTION
(15 to 20 minutes)

STOOPING DOWN

Arrange ahead of time with a preschool, kindergarten or first-grade teacher to have your kids visit his or her class briefly during this lesson. If a class isn't available to visit, skip the first part of this activity and ask the questions that follow based on what teenagers have observed in the past about preschoolers.

Give kids each a 3×5 card and a pencil. Say: **We're going to visit a children's class in progress. Try not to distract the kids while you observe them. As you watch the kids, make notes about what you see them do. List actions, emotions and any other observations you might have.**

Take the teenagers to the prearranged class or classes. After three to five minutes, have your students return to your classroom.

Have kids tell what they observed about the children.

Then ask:

● **What's difficult about observing the children from a distance?** (You don't really know what they're thinking; it's tough to learn much about them.)

● **Did you fully appreciate how the children felt and what they thought just by observing them? Explain.** (No, we could only see what we thought they felt; yes, I could remember when I was a child and what it felt like.)

Pull out the children's toys and give them to the class members. Ask students to become like children and play for a few minutes with the toys. Encourage class members to sit on the floor or walk on their knees to help them get the proper perspective. Girls in dresses might choose to sit at chairs and play with the toys. Also, have kids talk as if they were children, using only simple words and sentences.

After a few minutes, collect the toys and ask:

● **How did you feel playing with children's toys?** (It was fun; I was embarrassed; I felt like a kid.)

● **What did you discover about children by becoming like a child?** (Adults look like giants to kids; children must get tired of playing with the same toys all the time.)

● **How is the information you learned while "being" children different from what you learned while observing children?** (Being children taught us more; observing children wasn't as valuable.)

● **How is becoming like children in this activity like the way God became human in Jesus?** (By becoming human, God knew humans better; God became human so we could understand him better.)

● **What benefits do we gain from God becoming human?** (We got to know God better; we are able to relate to God better.)

Say: **In our activity, you didn't actually become children, you simply acted like them. Yet God, in his ultimate power and wisdom, actually became human in Jesus Christ. Let's explore what it means for God to become human.**

MAKING THE WORD COME ALIVE

Have kids sit in a circle and each put on a blindfold. Say: **I'm going to give some of you items to describe to the rest of the class. When I give the item to you, take a few seconds to describe the object without naming it or saying what it's used for. You may not know what it is, and that's okay.**

Give someone in the circle an item from a box of miscellaneous items. Your box might include things such as paper clips, key rings, pencils, bottle caps or other, more obscure, items such as parts from toasters, stereos or other mechanical items.

Allow the volunteer up to 20 seconds to describe his or her item. Then say: **Before I pass this item around, make a mental snapshot of what you think it looks and feels like.**

Pause, then have the volunteer pass the item around. Repeat this activity as time permits so other kids can attempt to describe items.

After volunteers have described their items and passed them around, have kids remove their blindfolds.

Ask:

● **How did you feel as you tried to describe the item you were holding?** (Frustrated; confident; unsure.)

● **How did your mental picture of each item change when you got to hold the item?** (I discovered what was being described; I understood better.)

Read aloud John 1:1-18.

BIBLE APPLICATION
(15 to 20 minutes)

Ask:
● **How is what God did by becoming flesh like what you did when you held the items from our last activity in your hands?** (God became someone we could better understand; God became flesh so we could relate to him.)

Have kids place the items from this activity in the center of the circle. Have kids in turn choose one item from the pile and explain how it represents something about Jesus as human or divine. For example, someone who picks up a pencil might say, "If Jesus walked the earth today, he could actually use this pencil," or "Jesus has the power to create the tree that this pencil was made from, but he chose to walk among the trees with us." Encourage kids to be creative in their descriptions of Jesus.

Say: **As we explore what the Bible says about Jesus, we may discover more questions than answers. Don't be afraid to ask your questions and dig deeper. The more we learn about Jesus, the more we'll want to know.**

COMMITMENT
(5 to 10 minutes)

I STILL HAVE QUESTIONS

Give each student a pencil and a sheet of paper. Have kids each tear their paper into a question mark shape. Say: **On your question mark, write your name, then complete the following sentences:**
● **If Jesus is truly God and truly man, that means I . . .**
● **A question that I still have about Jesus is . . .**
● **One thing I can do to get to know Jesus better is . . .**

Form groups of no more than five, and have kids share what they wrote on their question marks. Then have students each say one thing they appreciate about what the others in their group wrote. For example, someone might say, "I really like the question you came up with about Jesus," or "Your idea on how to get to know Jesus better is a good one."

When all have finished, tape the question marks on a wall and leave them up for the duration of this course.

Table Talk

The Table Talk activity in this course helps senior highers talk with their parents about who Jesus is.

If you choose to use the Table Talk activity, this is a good time to show students the "Table Talk" handout (p. 18). Ask them to spend time with their parents completing it.

Before kids leave, give them each the "Table Talk" handout to take home, or tell them you'll be sending it to their parents. Tell kids to be prepared to report on their experience with the handout next week.

Or use the Table Talk idea found in the Bonus Ideas (p. 46) for a meeting based on the handout.

☐ OPTION 1: JOYFUL NOISE

Say: **Because only God is God, we can't fully understand Jesus' divine nature and what it meant for him to be God. But because we are human, we can understand what Jesus felt when he walked the earth many years ago. Prayerfully consider the powerful message God gave us when he became human in Jesus while the music plays. When the song is over, so is our class.**

Play a quiet song on a tape player while kids spend time in prayer. Or, if your group enjoys singing, consider singing together a song such as "Open Our Eyes" by Bob Cull. You can find this song and many others in *The Group Songbook* (Group Books).

☐ OPTION 2: JUST LIKE ME

Read aloud Luke 24:36-49. Form groups of no more than six and have kids each sit in a circle in their group and put on their blindfolds. Say: **I'm going to pass a piece of modeling clay around the circle to my right. I'll first shape it to represent how I feel about Jesus before passing it around. When you receive the clay, use your fingers to examine the shape, then pray silently for the person who handed you the clay. Then reshape the clay to represent how you feel about Jesus and pass it to the next person. We'll continue this until each person has prayed for the person on the left and reshaped the clay.**

Play quiet music while the clay is passed around the circle. When the clay returns to you, say "Amen" and dismiss the class.

CLOSING
(up to 5 minutes)

If You Still Have Time . . .

Other Views—Invite your pastor to talk about religious groups that have a different viewpoint about Jesus' humanity or divinity. Or, simply have kids discuss the following questions:
- If you have faith in God, does it really matter what you believe about Jesus? Explain.
- What's wrong with groups that believe Jesus was a great teacher, but not God?
- Why is it important that Jesus was both God and human?

Dramatic Picture—Have kids create and perform a short skit or drama based on Luke 24:36-49 and discuss it afterward.

Table Talk

To the Parent: We're involved in a high school course at church called *Who Is Jesus?* We'd like you and your teenager to spend some time discussing this important topic. Use this "Table Talk" page to help you do that.

Parent and senior higher

Take turns completing the following sentences:

- When I think of Jesus, I think of . . .
- Most of what I've learned about Jesus I learned from . . .
- Jesus is my friend because . . .
- Faith in Christ means . . .
- Jesus' death and Resurrection are important because . . .

Choose two of the following descriptive words about Jesus that are most important to you. Then talk with each other about your choices and explain why you chose what you did.

● Savior	● Friend	● Life	● Mediator
● Redeemer	● Teacher	● Door	● Lord
● Shepherd	● Truth	● Healer	● Way

Read and respond to the following:

- Why is Jesus' humanity important to you?
- Why is Jesus' divinity important to you?
- How much time do you spend each week talking with a close friend? with Jesus? How can you spend more time talking with Jesus?
- What's the greatest lesson you've learned from Jesus?
- What questions do you still have about Jesus?

Read together John 1:1-18. Discuss what these verses mean to you.

WHO IS JESUS?

MY BEST FRIEND

From Jesus, our best friend, springs every other love. Best friends stay together even when the bottom of life is collapsing. This was Jesus' promise: "I will be with you always" to laugh, play, work, cry, eat, sigh, and celebrate, and to talk to every day. That's what makes best friends.

To help senior highers see Jesus as a friend who desires to walk with them daily.

LESSON AIM

Students will:
- **discover the qualities of a best friend;**
- **see Jesus as a best friend;**
- **commit to specific steps of growing deeper in a friendship with Jesus; and**
- **share a friendship word with a friend.**

OBJECTIVES

Look up the following scripture. Then read the background paragraphs to see how the passage relates to your senior highers.

In **John 15:9-17**, Jesus describes the true meaning of love for a friend.

Jesus displays the most radical friendship by laying down his life for "his friends," literally "the ones he loves." Jesus magnified the normal, everyday use of the word "friend" by his sacrificial act. Yet Jesus' friendship does not require our obedience.

Jesus calls us friends. And friendship means more than just doing one's duty—it means an intimate relationship. Teenagers can discover that relationship as they learn about the qualities of friendship Jesus exemplified. And by developing a closer friendship with Jesus, teenagers can learn how to *be* better friends.

BIBLE BASIS
JOHN 15:9-17

Section	Minutes	What Students Will Do	Supplies
Opener (Option 1)	5 to 10	**Friendship Race**—Compete in a race to gain new friends.	
(Option 2)		**Friendship Symbols**—Create symbols representing friendship.	Pipe cleaners
Action and Reflection	10 to 15	**Friendship Auction**—Try to "win" friendship traits.	"Friendship Traits" hand-outs (p. 25), pencils
Bible Application	15 to 20	**Friendship Cards From Jesus**—Give each other cards of encouragement as if written by jesus.	Paper, markers, Bibles, "Friendship Bible Passages" handouts (p. 26)
Commitment	5 to 10	**Getting to Know a Friend**—Spend a few minutes getting to know someone in class.	
Closing (Option 1)	up to 5	**Friend to Friend**—Participate in a group prayer and thank Jesus for being a friend.	
(Option 2)		**Friends Forever**—Brainstorm things that make friendships last.	Bibles

The Lesson

OPTION 1: FRIENDSHIP RACE

Ask for two or three volunteers. If your group is larger than 12, ask for one volunteer for every four people in your class. Say: **We're going to see which of these volunteers can gain the most friends within four minutes. The rules of this activity are simple: The volunteers may use any means necessary to gain friendships with the other class members. For example, they may attempt to bribe people, give them compliments or simply be nice to them. After time is up, I'll ask class members to choose which one volunteer they'll be friends with. For this activity, ignore how you feel about the people in real life and base your decision solely on the next four minutes. Ready? Go.**

After four minutes, call time. Have class members each go and stand next to the volunteer they choose to be friends with. This activity may bring out feelings of unpopularity in volunteers. Remind kids this is just an exercise, but be prepared to talk to kids about their feelings if they seem upset by the outcome of the game.

Ask:

OPENER
(5 to 10 minutes)

● **How did you feel as the volunteers tried to make you their friends?** (Uncomfortable; it was fun; unsure.)

● **How is that like or unlike the way people become friends in real life?** (It's different because friends aren't made in just four minutes; it's similar because friends are created through common interests.)

● **What methods did volunteers use to develop friendships?** (Bribing; being kind; telling about a common interest; saying nice things.)

● **What are the best ways to develop friendships?** (Spend time together; ask lots of questions about the other person.)

Say: **In this activity, it might've been fun to bribe people into being your friend. But in reality, building a friendship goes much deeper than material goods or a common interest. Today we'll explore the importance of friendship with each other and with someone who wants to be our best friend—Jesus.**

☐ OPTION 2: FRIENDSHIP SYMBOLS

Form groups of no more than five. Give groups each a supply of pipe cleaners. Say: **In the next three minutes, talk with your group members about what you could make with your pipe cleaners. You can use the pipe cleaners with any other item in the room except another group's pipe cleaners.**

The object you create must somehow represent something about friendship. For example, you could create something as simple as a heart shape with your pipe cleaners to represent the love friends have for each other. Make sure each person in your group helps with this project.

Allow a few minutes for groups to create their items. Then have groups each describe what they created.

Ask:

● **How did you feel about working together in your group to create these friendship symbols?** (Frustrated; confident; valuable.)

● **How is this like the way people feel when they're developing friendships?** (They feel listened to; they feel frustrated sometimes; they feel valuable.)

● **What positive things did you learn about the people in your group through working together on this activity?**

Say: **Working together is one way of developing a friendship with someone. By spending time together working toward a common goal, you can discover much about other people. Today we're going to examine how we can get to know Jesus better as our friend—and how a friendship with Jesus can help us become better friends with others.**

Table Talk Follow-Up

If you sent the "Table Talk" handout (p. 18) to parents last week, discuss students' reactions to the activity. Ask volunteers to share what they learned from the discussion with their parents.

ACTION AND REFLECTION

(10 to 15 minutes)

FRIENDSHIP AUCTION

Give kids each a pencil and a photocopy of the "Friendship Traits" handout (p. 25). Say: **In a couple minutes, you'll have the opportunity to "win" some of the traits described on this handout.**

The object of this activity is to win as many of these traits as possible. The way you do this is by demonstrating the trait you want to as many people as possible during the time available. Once you've demonstrated that trait, the person you're demonstrating it to must sign his or her name next to the item on your handout. But the trick is that you may not say which trait you're demonstrating. You may speak, but not specifically about the trait you're going after. Remember that integrity is one of these items—so don't cheat.

When time is up, we'll see who has the most signatures for each item. Choose the traits you think are most important.

Give kids a couple minutes to read the handout. Then, on "go," have teenagers go around demonstrating friendship traits to each other.

After about five minutes, call time and have kids sit in a circle. Read each item on the handout and find out who has the most signatures for that item.

Then ask:

● **How did you feel as you demonstrated friendship traits to each other?** (It was fun; I felt good; I liked it; I felt uncomfortable.)

● **How did you feel as you were shown friendship traits by others?** (I felt good; I liked it.)

● **How is this like the way you feel when someone reaches out to you in friendship?** (I feel good when I get a new friend; I feel good when I get to know someone better.)

● **How important are friendships? Explain.** (Very important, friends help you feel valuable; somewhat important, it's more important to know who you are than to have lots of friends.)

● **What qualities do great friends have?** (Patience; a caring attitude; love; concern; helpfulness.)

Say: **Many of the friendship traits you described and practiced are traits shown by Jesus. We often think of Jesus as someone who lived "back then" or as God's son. But he's also someone who simply wants to be close to** you and support you. Let's take a few minutes to explore examples of Jesus' reaching out to us in friendship.

FRIENDSHIP CARDS FROM JESUS

Say: **Best friends say encouraging and supporting words when they're working together toward a goal. They celebrate the joys of their triumphs and hold onto each other when things are falling to pieces. According to this definition, Jesus must then be our best friend.**

Give kids each two or three sheets of paper, a marker, a Bible and a photocopy of the "Friendship Bible Passages" handout (p. 26). Say: **Choose at least two passages from the "Friendship Bible Passages" handout and read them. Then design your own "Friendship Card From Jesus" based on the meaning of that passage.**

For example, if you read John 10:14-15, you might design a card with sheep on the front and a message on the inside describing how much Jesus cares for you. Word the message as if Jesus were writing this card to you. Here's an example from the John 10:14-15 passage:

I would lay down my life for you . . . in fact, I did!

You are that important to me. I love you! Your Best Friend, Jesus

Allow a few minutes for teenagers to read the Bible passages and create "Friendship Cards From Jesus." Then form pairs and have kids each give their card or cards to their partner and say why that person is "worth it" as a friend. Ask teenagers to talk about the message in the cards and why it's important to see Jesus as a friend.

Have partners briefly discuss the following questions:

● **How does it feel to know Jesus is your friend?**

● **How can we be more like Jesus in our relationships with our friends?**

Have a volunteer read aloud John 15:9-17.

Ask:

● **How does this passage make you feel?** (Uncomfortable; unworthy; surprised.)

● **Would it be easy to lay your life down for a friend? Why or why not?** (Yes, I love my friends; no, I don't think I could do that.)

GETTING TO KNOW A FRIEND

Have kids each pair up with the person they know the least. Say: **As we discover a close friendship with Jesus, we learn more about how we can be friends with others. During the next three minutes, talk with your partner about anything you'd like to talk about, such as where you were born, what you like to do in your free time, and what your biggest dream for the future is. But as you talk, remember to be patient, caring, supportive and to exhibit**

BIBLE APPLICATION
(15 to 20 minutes)

COMMITMENT
(5 to 10 minutes)

other traits that make a good friend. Use this time to get to know your partner better.

After three minutes, call time and have kids form a circle. Ask:

● **How did you feel about spending time with your partner?** (Good; uncomfortable; fine.)

● **How is this like or unlike how you might feel about getting to know Jesus as a friend?** (I'd feel uncomfortable; I'd feel fine.)

Say: **Jesus wants to be our friend. But we may feel uncomfortable opening up our lives to him. One of the best ways to get to know Jesus better is to read the Bible.**

Meet again with your partner and write a statement of commitment on the back of your "Friendship Bible Passages" handout, stating what you'll do to get to know Jesus better in the coming weeks. Then sign your commitment and have your partner sign it, to seal your desire to grow closer to Jesus as a friend.

☐ OPTION 1: FRIEND TO FRIEND

Form a circle. Have kids each take a turn saying a short prayer for the person on their left. Then, have kids repeat after you in unison: **Thank you for giving us friends we can talk to,** (pause) **lean on,** (pause) **support** (pause) **and grow close to. And thank you for your friendship** (pause). **In Jesus' name, amen.**

☐ OPTION 2: FRIENDS FOREVER

Form pairs. Have partners each say at least one thing they believe makes friendships last, such as honesty, patience and love. Then have kids each pray that their partner exhibits those qualities in their own friendships.

Close by reading John 3:16 and John 15:13 to remind kids about Jesus' ultimate act of friendship.

CLOSING
(up to 5 minutes)

If You Still Have Time . . .

Footwashing—Have a couple of pans of warm water and towels available for the students to wash each other's feet. After the experience, have kids discuss how they felt serving each other.

Ask:

● What role does serving play in friendships?

● How easy is it to serve your friends?

Have kids read and discuss John 13:1-17.

Ask:

● What can we learn from Jesus' serving attitude?

Best Friends—Have kids each write a short poem about their best friend or what it takes to be a best friend. Then have teenagers each read aloud their poem. Afterward, have kids discuss what it means to be a best friend.

FRIENDSHIP TRAITS

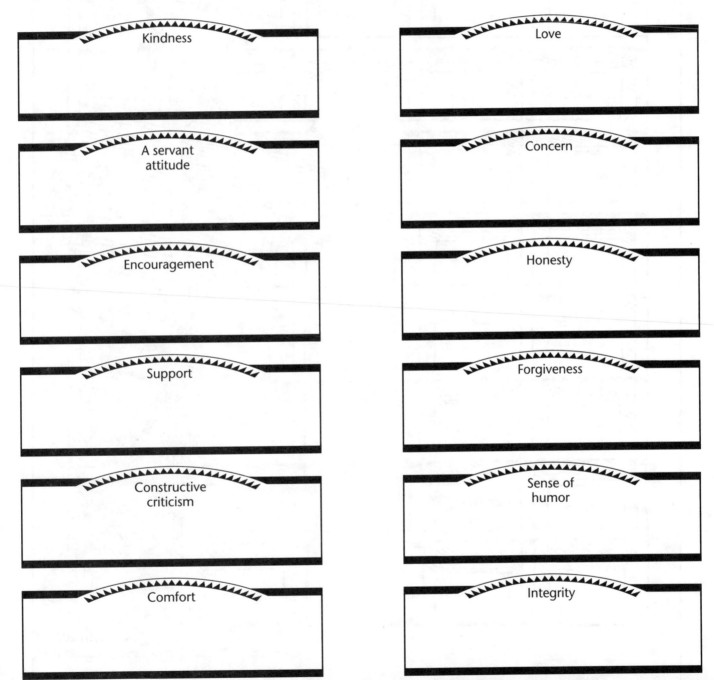

Kindness

Love

A servant attitude

Concern

Encouragement

Honesty

Support

Forgiveness

Constructive criticism

Sense of humor

Comfort

Integrity

Friendship Bible Passages

Choose one or more
of the following passages to read
and use to create "Friendship Cards From Jesus."

John 3:16-17   John 4:13-14   John 5:6-9   John 5:24

John 6:16-20   John 6:35   John 8:6-11   John 8:12

John 8:31-36   John 9:1-7

John 10:9-10   John 10:14-15   John 10:27-30

John 11:35-36   John 11:25-27   John 13:1-9

John 14:1-6   John 14:12-14   John 14:15-21   John 14:26-27

John 15:5   John 15:9-17   John 16:20-22   John 16:23-24

John 17:20-23   John 20:19-23   John 20:29   John 21:15-17

BEHOLD THE TEACHER

For most students, the popularity of a class at school is influenced by the relationship kids have with the teacher. If the teacher shows genuine concern for the students, respects them and values their opinions, the students often will work harder and want to learn more. A teacher who loves the students and shows them practical application of the subject will help students grow. Jesus is a loving teacher. And teenagers can learn to respect and grow from his teaching.

To help senior highers see Jesus as the master teacher.

LESSON AIM

Students will:
● **discover a new perspective on things around them;**
● **learn how Jesus taught his disciples;**
● **explore how to learn from Jesus' teachings; and**
● **see Jesus as the master teacher of God's Word.**

OBJECTIVES

Look up the following scriptures. Then read the background paragraphs to see how the passages relate to your senior highers.

BIBLE BASIS
MATTHEW 7:28-29
MARK 4:1-2

Matthew 7:28-29 describes Jesus' authority as teacher.
Teaching is the principle activity Jesus engages in during his public ministry. Matthew cites Jesus as one who teaches, preaches and heals. John the Baptist and the disciples are also described as preachers, but teaching remains Jesus' special prerogative. And Jesus taught with authority that amazed the people.
Through the scriptures, teenagers can gain the same knowledge the disciples gained from Jesus. They can discover much

about God's will for their lives when they see Jesus as master teacher.

Mark 4:1-2 introduces a series of parables taught by Jesus. The collection of parables following this passage is addressed to crowds who would listen. These parables in Mark serve to help readers understand the whole gospel. And they relate Jesus' ministry to the kingdom of God.

Sometimes it's tough to unlock the meaning of the parables. Yet by struggling with Jesus' parables, teenagers can gain new insight into Jesus' life—and how they can live in the kingdom of God today.

THIS LESSON AT A GLANCE

Section	Minutes	What Students Will Do	Supplies
Opener (Option 1)	5 to 10	**Kingdom Balloons**—Create balloon collages representing the kingdom of God.	Balloons, tape, string, markers, magazines, pin
(Option 2)		**Parable Discovery**—Brainstorm what a parable is.	Newsprint, markers
Action and Reflection	15 to 20	**New Perspectives**—Explore new perspectives of their surroundings.	3×5 cards, nail
Bible Application	10 to 15	**Parable Views**—Discover how Jesus used parables to teach his disciples.	"Parable Views" handouts (p. 34), Bibles, pencils
Commitment	5 to 10	**Learning From the Teacher**—Commit to read and learn more about Jesus' teachings.	Paper, pencils
Closing (Option 1)	up to 5	**Jesus Is . . .**—Call out words describing Jesus.	Balloons, markers
(Option 2)		**Teacher, Teach Me**—Recite a closing prayer together.	Bibles

The Lesson

OPENER
(5 to 10 minutes)

☐ OPTION 1: KINGDOM BALLOONS

Form groups of no more than five and give each of them a supply of balloons, tape, string, markers and magazines. Say: **You have four minutes to create a balloon collage illustrating what you imagine the kingdom of God is like. Be creative and do your best to illustrate this concept.**

After four minutes, call time and have groups each present

their balloon collage. Then walk around to each group's collage and pop the balloons using a straight pin.

Kids may try to hide their balloons or keep you from popping them. That's okay, just tell kids it's important for you to pop their balloons.

Form a circle and place the remnants of the balloon collages in the center.

Ask:

● **How did you feel when you finished your balloon collage?** (Pleased; happy; fine.)

● **How did you feel when I popped your balloons?** (I was surprised; I was angry; I was unprepared.)

● **How is this like the way Jesus' disciples might have felt when Jesus taught them something new?** (They were surprised; they were unprepared.)

● **How has your collage representing the kingdom of God changed?** (It's deflated; it looks different now.)

Say: **Just as I went around and surprised you by changing your picture of the kingdom of God, Jesus often surprised his disciples and reshaped their picture of the kingdom of God. Jesus painted his picture of the kingdom of God through teaching parables. Today we'll get to know Jesus better as teacher through his parables. And we'll get a clearer picture of the kingdom of God.**

☐ OPTION 2: PARABLE DISCOVERY

Tape a sheet of newsprint to the wall. At the top of the newsprint, write "A parable is . . . " Have kids line up according to birthdays. Then give the first person in line a marker.

Say: **Go to the newsprint and complete the definition of what a parable is. If you aren't sure, make something up. Then the next person in line will go and add to or correct the definition. Each person must somehow improve on the definition on the newsprint.**

After kids have worked on the definition of the word "parable," form a circle. Have kids read the final definition of "parable." Then read the following definition aloud and have kids compare their definition to it: **A parable is a short, simple story, usually based on a familiar occurence, from which a moral or lesson may be drawn.**

Ask:

● **How did you feel as you tried to work on a definition of a parable?** (Unsure; confident; I didn't know what to write.)

● **How is that like Jesus' disciples might have felt when they were listening to Jesus' teaching through parables?** (Some didn't understand what he meant; some didn't feel sure about his message.)

● **How do you feel about the final definition you came up with?** (I don't like it; it's not right; too many people changed it.)

● **What did you discover about a parable through this**

activity? (I discovered parables are stories; I discovered parables were Jesus' way of teaching.)

Say: **Just as you may have discovered something through this exercise, Jesus' disciples discovered much about the kingdom of God through his parables. Today we'll learn about Jesus as teacher—and how Jesus' teaching helps us understand what it means to be in God's kingdom.**

NEW PERSPECTIVES

Have kids stand and make sure they have plenty of space between them. Say: **For the first part of this activity, you'll each get to be mimes. Before we begin, look quickly around the room at your surroundings** (pause). **Now, as I give you instructions, follow them as well as you can as a mime might. Don't worry about looking silly—everyone will be doing the same thing.**

Give each of the following instructions, one at a time, allowing kids to each complete them before moving on.

Use your hands to "feel" a box around where you stand. Carefully feel the front . . . the sides . . . and the back of the box. Then reach up and touch the top of the box.

Now, see if you can find a door in your box. When you discover one, open it and look through it at your surroundings. Notice the detail.

Now close your door and look for a window. Open it carefully and look out. Again, look for details you might've missed when you looked around before discovering the box around you.

Now close the window and look for a mirror in your box. Study your reflection in the mirror.

While kids are still in their "boxes," ask:

● **How do you feel as you stand in your boxes?** (Silly; confident; embarrassed.)

● **How is that like the way the disciples might've felt when Jesus was teaching them?** (They may have felt silly; they probably felt embarrassed.)

● **What new things did you notice as you looked out the door of your box?**

● **What new things did you notice as you looked out the window of your box?**

● **What new things did you notice as you looked in the mirror of your box?**

● **How do you feel about what you discovered in this activity?** (Bored; surprised; happy.)

● **How are your discoveries like the discoveries the disciples may have had while learning from Jesus?** (They were surprised about what they learned; they were happy to learn new things.)

Have kids each fold their "box" and put it away. Form a circle and say: **The box you were in is very much like the** parables Jesus told. Through his parables, Jesus provided a new look at the kingdom of God. His parables were stories the people could relate to. And these parables helped people focus on their lives and how well they were in tune with God.

Give kids each a 3×5 card. Go around and poke a hole in each student's card using a medium-size nail. Then say: **Take the next couple minutes to observe the detail in things in this room by looking at items through the hole in your card. Choose one item you discover and make a mental "snapshot" of the item. We'll share our snapshots in a couple minutes.**

After a couple minutes, have kids form groups of no more than four and tell what "picture" they took.

Then say: **Our "cameras" help us focus on the small details of life around us. Jesus' teaching can help us do the same thing. Let's explore how Jesus, the master teacher, taught his disciples and can teach us too.**

PARABLE VIEWS

Form groups of no more than three. Assign groups each one of the following passages: Matthew 13:33; Matthew 13:44; Matthew 13:45,46; Matthew 13:47-52; Mark 4:3-9, 13-20; Mark 4:26-29; Mark 4:30-32; Luke 12:13-21; Luke 15:3-7; Luke 19:11-27. It's okay if you don't use all the passages or if groups have duplicate passages.

Give kids each a "Parable Views" handout (p. 34), a Bible and a pencil.

Say: **The best way to get to know Jesus, the teacher, is to explore what he taught to his students. And since Jesus often used parables to teach his disciples, we'll each closely examine one of his parables and what it tells us today.**

Have groups each read their passage, then discuss and complete the handout based on the passage.

Then form a circle and have representatives from each group relate how they completed the handout.

Ask:

● **What did you discover about Jesus, the teacher?** (He challenged his students; he made his students think for themselves.)

● **How can we learn from Jesus' parables today?** (By reading and studying the Bible; by talking with Christian friends; by going to church; by praying.)

Say: **Today we've already learned how Jesus used parables to help his disciples understand the kingdom of God. But now we'll choose specific ways to learn more from the master teacher in the coming weeks.**

BIBLE APPLICATION
(10 to 15 minutes)

COMMITMENT
(5 to 10 minutes)

CLOSING
(up to 5 minutes)

LEARNING FROM THE TEACHER

Give kids each a sheet of paper and a pencil. Say: **Draw a picture symbolizing what Jesus might want to teach you today. For example, if you think Jesus would teach you to love your brother more, draw an illustration of a heart and your brother.**

After a few minutes, form pairs and have partners discuss their drawings and what they mean. Then have partners each choose one way they can learn from the teacher in the next week (such as read a passage of scripture or spend an hour talking about Jesus with a friend). Have partners acknowledge each other's commitment to follow-through on these ideas by signing each other's drawing. Then have teenagers each tell their partner one reason he or she can keep his or her commitment. For example, someone might say, "You can do this because you always follow through on things," or "I know you'll keep this commitment because you're sincere in what you say." Encourage kids to keep the drawings as reminders to seek Jesus' teachings each day.

Then form a circle. Say: **Learning from Jesus, the teacher, is an adventure. When we explore his lessons in the Bible, we can grow in faith. And just as Jesus' disciples were challenged to gain a new perspective on life, we too are challenged to see his kingdom with new eyes.**

☐ OPTION 1: JESUS IS . . .

Say: **As we learn from Jesus through his teaching, we grow closer to him. Jesus' parables may challenge us to change our perspectives, but his love will always shine through even the toughest lessons.**

Give kids each a balloon and a marker. Have kids blow up the balloons and write on them words describing Jesus. For example, kids might write "friend," "teacher" or "savior."

At the same time, have kids celebrate Jesus by hitting the balloons in the air and calling out the words they've written on them. Have kids continue to hit the balloons in the air and call out the words until you call "stop." Then allow the balloons to drop to the floor and have kids spend a moment in silent prayer, thanking God for Jesus' teachings and his love for each person.

☐ OPTION 2: TEACHER, TEACH ME

Give kids each the same translation of the Bible. Have kids each turn to Psalm 143:8-10 in their Bibles. Say: **As our closing prayer today, we'll read this passage together. When we finish, shake the hands of at least three other people while saying to them, "May Jesus be your teacher and your guide."**

If You Still Have Time . . .

Like Teacher Like Student—Have the students think of the attributes they admire about their favorite teacher at school. List these attributes on newsprint. Have kids vote on the qualities from the list they'd like to develop. Then have the class read Philippians 2:5-11 and discuss why humility is important for teachers.

Jesus in Your School—Have kids discuss the following questions:

● If Jesus were a teacher in your school, what question would you like to ask him?

● How would other kids react to Jesus' teaching style if he were in your school?

● What can today's teachers learn about teaching from Jesus?

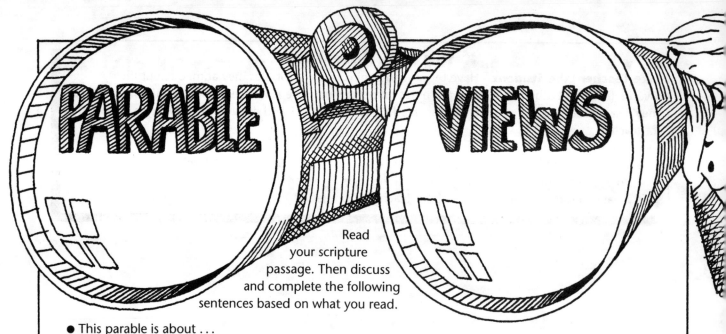

Read your scripture passage. Then discuss and complete the following sentences based on what you read.

● This parable is about . . .

● Jesus taught this parable because . . .

● A parable was a good way to teach this idea because . . .

● People today should listen to the message of this parable because . . .

● The new perspective this parable gives is . . .

Now read aloud Matthew 7:28-29 and Mark 4:1-2.

● What do these verses say about Jesus' teaching?

● What can we learn from Jesus' parables that can help us in everyday life?

● How do Jesus' parables help us understand God's kingdom?

MORE THAN CONQUERORS

Teenagers believe they are invincible. Yet the signs of death are all around them: suicide, drugs, murder, AIDS, anorexia, gangs, war, poverty, hunger. Teenagers begin to question what life is all about. And their questions reveal their fear of the unknown.

But kids can discover hope and confidence as they learn about Jesus' victory over death.

To help senior highers understand the impact of Jesus' victory over death.

LESSON AIM

Students will:
- celebrate Christ's victory;
- examine the meaning of Jesus' sacrificial death on the cross; and
- commit to grow in Christ.

OBJECTIVES

Look up the following scriptures. Then read the background paragraphs to see how the passages relate to your senior highers.

In **John 20:19-31**, Jesus appears to the disciples after his Resurrection.

Thomas had started down the road to unbelief and Jesus wanted to change that. But Jesus didn't put down Thomas because of his struggle with doubt. Rather Jesus celebrated Thomas' statement of faith.

Teenagers will probably doubt their faith more than once during their life. This passage helps teenagers see that even in their doubt, Jesus loves them and wants them to believe.

Romans 6:1-14 describes Jesus' victory over death.

This passage tells how Christ has freed us from the burden

BIBLE BASIS

JOHN 20:19-31
ROMANS 6:1-14
ROMANS 8:31-39

of carrying our signs of death—our sins. This freedom changes us from the moment we accept it. These verses describe the nature and manner of life that belongs to the people of God. It's a lesson on how to live and grow in a dying world.

Teenagers can discover from this passage how Jesus conquered death—and what that means for them today. Kids can learn how they can be conquerors over sin through Jesus Christ.

In **Romans 8:31-39**, Paul explains that if God is for us, then no one can defeat us.

In this passage Paul describes life with Christ in a jubilant song of praise. He describes how we're more than conquerors. We belong to God, who is for us. Nothing can separate us from Jesus' love.

This is the ultimate encouragement for young Christians who aren't sure about their faith. Paul's words can both comfort and challenge teenagers as they see the power of Jesus' love for them.

THIS LESSON AT A GLANCE

Section	Minutes	What Students Will Do	Supplies
Opener (Option 1)	5 to 10	**Victory**—Play a game and talk about how it feels to win.	Wastebasket, paper, doughnuts
(Option 2)		**Here Lies . . .**—Design their gravestones.	Black paper, chalk
Action and Reflection	10 to 15	**Scapegoat**—Discover how Jesus was the scapegoat for our sins.	Chairs
Bible Application	15 to 20	**Victory Parties**—Create parties based on themes in Romans.	Confetti, balloons, Bibles
Commitment	5 to 10	**Faith Vitality**—Evaluate their level of faith and commit to find ways to grow closer to Jesus.	"Faith Vitality" handouts (p. 42), pencils
Closing (Option 1)	up to 5	**Feed My Sheep**—Describe who Jesus is.	
(Option 2)		**Takin' It to the Streets**—Brainstorm ways to tell others about Jesus.	Newsprint, marker

The Lesson

☐ OPTION 1: VICTORY

Set up a "basketball" court by placing empty wastebaskets at either end of the room. Then form two teams. If your group is larger than 10, form four teams and place two additional wastebaskets against the two other walls of the room.

Say: **The object of this game is to get the most crumpled papers into your wastebasket. You'll need to position your team members in the room before we begin. Once play starts, you may not move. I'll toss in a crumpled sheet of paper and you may then try to shoot or block the paper until someone makes a basket. You may not grab the paper out of anyone else's hands. If the paper lands too far away for anyone to reach, I'll get it and put it into play again.**

Play for five minutes or so. After time is up, count the number of papers in each wastebasket to determine the winner. Give the winning team a prize of a box of doughnuts.

Form a circle and ask the winning team:
● **How did it feel to win?** (Good; exciting; great.)

Ask everyone:
● **How do you feel when you win a competition?** (Great; happy; proud.)
● **How is that like the way we can feel knowing that Jesus "won" the battle over death?** (We can feel great; we can feel happy about Jesus' victory.)

Say: **Winning a game of basketball is a small victory. But Jesus' victory over death is the ultimate victory. Today we're going to explore how Jesus conquered death and what that means for us.**

Give the rest of the students doughnuts too.

☐ OPTION 2: HERE LIES . . .

Give teenagers each a sheet of black paper and a piece of chalk. Have students use the paper and chalk to design their own gravestone. Say: **On your gravestone, draw a symbol that represents something important about you. Then write your epitaph, a statement describing how you'd like to be remembered.**

After a few minutes, have kids each stand in front of the group and read aloud their gravestone and describe the symbol on it.

Then form a circle and ask:
● **How did you feel when you were reading your epitaph to the whole class?** (It felt funny; I didn't like it; I felt uncomfortable.)

OPENER
(5 to 10 minutes)

● **How is this like the way people feel about the topic of death?** (People don't like to talk about death; people are uncomfortable talking about death.)

● **Why is it difficult to talk about death?** (People are afraid of death; death is an unknown.)

● **Why are people afraid of death?** (Because they don't know what happens at death; because they aren't sure about their faith.)

Say: **Death isn't an easy subject to discuss. But we can be thankful because Jesus has conquered death, and we can celebrate his victory together. This lesson will help us see what Jesus' victory over death means for our lives.**

SCAPEGOAT

Set up a bunch of folding chairs in the room. You'll need one for each person in your class. Choose a song your group knows well. Say: **We're going to sing a song together as we march with these chairs around the room. Each person must carry a chair at arm's length. Keep singing and walking around the room and follow the instructions I give.**

Choose a volunteer and ask him or her to be prepared to help out during the song. The volunteer should join in with the singing just like everyone else.

Have kids begin marching around the room as they carry the chairs at arm's length. The chairs will probably begin to get heavy. As you see kids struggle with the weight of the chair, tell them to give their chairs to the volunteer. By the end of the song, the volunteer should be holding all of the chairs (or be buried under the chairs if you have a large group). Have the volunteer silently remain where he or she is—while still burdened or buried by the chairs.

Have kids sit in a circle around the volunteer and sing another song such as "He Is Lord" or "I Love You, Lord." Encourage kids to be prayerful and serious during this song.

Then ask:

● **How did you feel as you carried your chair around the room?** (It got heavy; I felt uncomfortable.)

● **How is that like the way you feel when you sin against God?** (I feel like a weight is on my shoulders; I feel bad.)

● **How did you feel when you could give away your chair?** (I felt relieved; I felt free; I felt good; I felt bad for the volunteer.)

● **How is the way the volunteer took your chairs like the way Jesus took away our sins?** (Jesus died for each of our sins.)

Say: **A scapegoat is a person who takes the blame for others' mistakes.**

Ask the volunteer:

● **How did it feel to be the scapegoat?** (I didn't like it; it was tough.)

ACTION AND REFLECTION

(10 to 15 minutes)

● **How might that be like how Jesus felt?** (Jesus probably felt like it was difficult to be the scapegoat; Jesus knew he didn't have a choice.)

Say: **This past four weeks we've been discovering who Jesus is. But this lesson is probably the most important as we explore the nature of Jesus. Jesus became our savior when he took upon himself all of our sins. And we can be thankful because he conquered death, which opened up our line of communication with God once again. Because of Jesus' sacrifice, we can now overcome death, too, and live with God for all eternity.**

Yet it's sometimes difficult to believe Jesus actually conquered death.

VICTORY PARTIES

Form two groups. Make sure each group has a Bible. Give groups each one of the following passages: Romans 6:1-14 or Romans 8:31-39. Then give groups each a supply of confetti and balloons. Say: **In your group, read the passage and discuss what implications it has for our lives today. Then create a party theme based on what you discover. In a few minutes, you'll throw your party for the other group.**

Go around and help groups find the joyful message in each passage. For the Romans 6:1-14 passage, kids might come up with a theme of "Victory in Christ." For the Romans 8:31-39 passage, kids might come up with a theme of "More Than Conquerors" or "Nothing Can Separate Us From God." Encourage groups to each come up with a chant or rap describing the meaning of their passage.

After about five minutes, have groups each describe the theme of their party, do their chant or rap, and toss confetti and balloons to celebrate the message of their passage.

Then ask:

● **How did you feel as you celebrated your scripture passage?** (Great; happy; excited.)

● **How is that like the way we feel, knowing that Jesus overcame death?** (It's exciting that Jesus died and rose again for us; it makes me feel happy that Jesus loves me enough to die for me.)

Say: **It's exciting to think about the impact of Jesus' victory over death. But sometimes our faith wavers as we think about who Jesus is.**

Read aloud John 20:19-31 while volunteers act out the parts of Jesus, Thomas and the other disciples.

Then ask:

● **Have you ever felt like Thomas? Explain.** (Yes, sometimes I doubt my faith; no, I trust that Jesus rose from the dead.)

● **How does the message of John 20:29 make you feel?** Read the verse aloud again. (Since I've not seen Jesus, my faith must be strong; I think I'd rather actually see Jesus

---

BIBLE APPLICATION
(15 to 20 minutes)

than be blessed for having faith without seeing him.)

Say: **Our faith is sometimes shaken by our doubts. That's pretty normal. Yet, with continued support from friends, Christian leaders and the work of the Holy Spirit, we can grow stronger in faith.**

COMMITMENT
(5 to 10 minutes)

FAITH VITALITY

Give kids each a "Faith Vitality" handout (p. 42) and a pencil. Have teenagers complete the handout, then meet with a partner to discuss how they feel about the completed handout. Tell kids they don't have to reveal their answers to their partner.

Then have kids say one way they'll improve their faith vitality during the coming weeks. Have teenagers then tell their partners why they think they'll be successful in this goal. For example, if a teenager says, "I'll study the Bible three times a week," his or her partner might add, "I know you can do that because you're good at following through with things."

Then form a circle and have kids each tell the whole group what they're planning to do during the coming weeks to strengthen their faith.

Say: **Our faith will grow as we discover more about Jesus. This past four weeks we've only begun to see the impact Jesus has on our lives. In the weeks to come, continue to seek new understanding of how Jesus fits in your life—and how you can be more like him.**

CLOSING
(up to 5 minutes)

☐ OPTION 1: FEED MY SHEEP

Have teenagers sit in a circle. One at a time ask them to answer the following question: **(Name), who do you say this Jesus is?** After each person answers the question, say: **Then feed his sheep.** For example, kids might answer by saying, "He is a friend," or "He is the savior."

After the last person responds, join hands and all shout together, "Amen!"

☐ OPTION 2: TAKIN' IT TO THE STREETS

Say: **The more we discover about who Jesus is, the more we realize we must tell this news to others. Jesus commands us to go out and spread the "good news" of his victory over death to all the nations.**

Have teenagers brainstorm a list of ways they can tell others about who Jesus is and what he means to them. Have a volunteer write the ideas on a sheet of newsprint taped to a wall. For example, kids might suggest, "Tell a friend who's depressed about the joy Jesus brings," or "Ask a friend what he or she believes about Jesus—then describe what you believe."

Close by having kids each sign the list and silently commit to using one of the ideas during the coming week. Keep the newsprint list in your room for a few weeks as a reminder to tell others about who Jesus is.

If You Still Have Time . . .

I Am—Have someone read aloud John 8:28. Then have kids search the Gospel of John for all the "I am" statements and list them on individual cards. One at a time, have kids read aloud the cards, then toss them into the air. Have students discuss how these statements free us.

Course Reflection—Form a circle. Ask students to reflect on the past four lessons. Have them take turns completing the following sentences:

- Something I learned in this course was . . .
- If I could tell my friends about this course, I'd say . . .
- Something I'll do differently because of this course is . . .

FAITH VITALITY

Rate the vitality of your faith life for each item below from 1 (barely breathing) to 10 (you feel like you could walk on water).

Today, I'd rate my faith vitality as a . . .

1   2   3   4   5   6   7   8   9   10

I wish my faith vitality would be a . . .

1   2   3   4   5   6   7   8   9   10

When I'm with my Christian friends, my faith vitality is usually a . . .

1   2   3   4   5   6   7   8   9   10

When I'm with friends who don't know I'm a Christian, my faith vitality is usually a . . .

1   2   3   4   5   6   7   8   9   10

Now complete the following sentences:
I live out my faith by doing the following:

If I want my faith vitality to move up on the scale, I'll need to stop . . .

If I want my faith vitality to move up on the scale, I'll need to start . . .

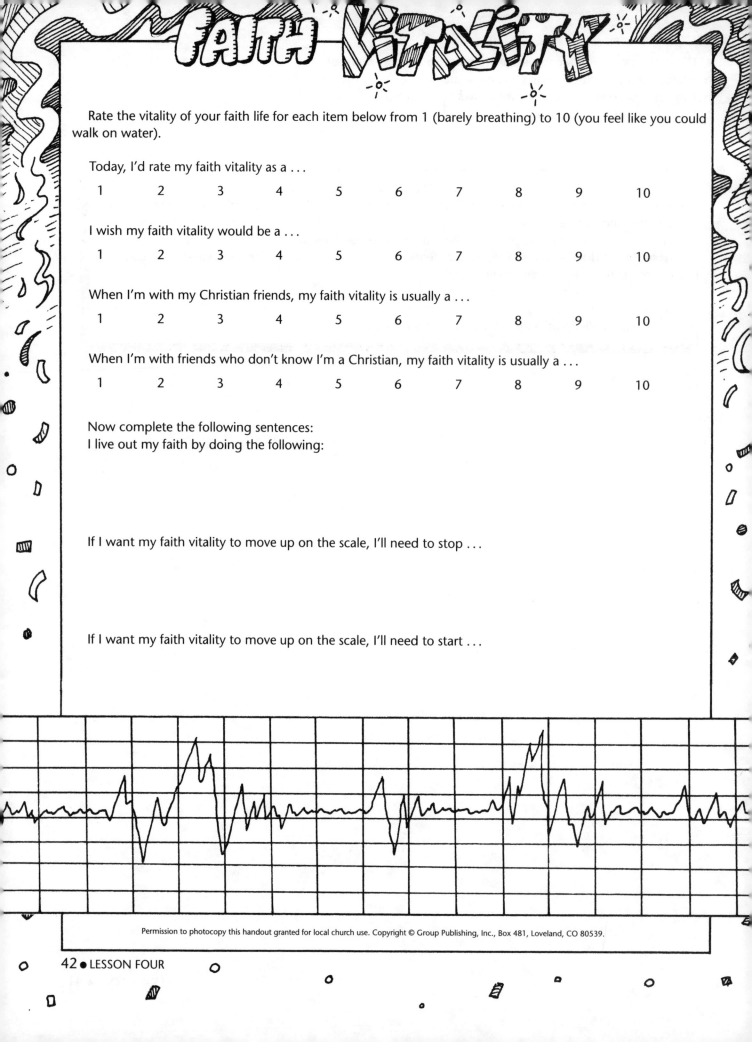

BONUS IDEAS

Traditional Teaching—Visit a synagogue or invite a local rabbi to visit your class and share with you the traditional teaching style of a rabbi. Have kids discuss how they would've felt growing up in Jesus' time with this style of teaching. Have kids ask the rabbi why Judaism doesn't recognize Jesus as the messiah.

Thanks!—Have kids each write a thank-you note to someone who has helped them understand who Jesus is. Encourage kids to choose people who have helped them grow in faith. Then have kids deliver their notes to the appropriate people.

In His Footsteps—Have kids help you cut footprints out of colorful paper. Then have kids each write their statement of faith and their name on a footprint. Ask kids to discuss how faith is a way of walking in Jesus' footsteps. Then tape up the footprints in a hallway in your church where others can see them.

Who is Jesus? Survey—Place a box with an opening cut in the top at the back of your church one Sunday. During the service, have teenagers hand out 3×5 cards to congregation members to use in answering the question, "Who is Jesus to you?" Then have congregation members drop the cards into the box after the service.

Plan a meeting where kids can read the cards and discuss them. For fun, have kids use the cards and colorful decorations to create a mural in the church. Have kids "introduce" the mural to the church the following Sunday.

In-Depth Study—Have kids explore a deeper understanding of who Jesus is by inviting a senior pastor to lead them in a Bible study of Jesus' parables or some other aspect of Jesus' life.

Jesus in the Media—Have kids research how Jesus is depicted in television, movies and music. Suggest kids keep a journal of references to Jesus that they hear or see over a one-month period. Then meet to discuss how the media world portrays Jesus and how they feel about that.

Jesus, Movie Star?—Rent and watch *Jesus Christ Superstar* with your kids. Afterward, have kids compare the story of Jesus' life with the accounts in the gospels. Ask kids to evaluate the accuracy and value of the movie.

MEETINGS AND MORE

Table Talk—Use the Table Talk handout (p. 18) as the basis for a meeting with parents and teenagers. During the meeting, have parents and kids complete the handout and discuss it. Open the meeting with a time for crowdbreakers and fun games to help parents and kids feel comfortable with each other. Use ideas from *Have-a-Blast Games* (Group Books).

During the meeting, have parents tell how their faith has developed since they were in high school.

PARTY PLEASER

Songfest—Help kids plan a party based on listening to and singing songs about Jesus. Check out *The Group Songbook* (Group Publishing) for songs to sing and your local Christian bookstore for tapes or CDs with songs about Jesus. During the party, have trivia games based on Jesus' miracles. And plan lots of fun foods for kids to enjoy.

RETREAT IDEA

In Jesus' Time—Have kids help you plan a retreat designed to take kids back to Jesus' time. Work with volunteers to create a retreat environment that matches the lifestyle and culture of the first century. Check out books on biblical history to get ideas for decorating the retreat site and for fun food ideas.

During the retreat, have kids dress up as Jesus' disciples. Focus the retreat on understanding who Jesus is. You might want to use activities from the four lessons that you didn't use during the Sunday school time.

Help kids explore the impact Jesus had on his disciples and how they can feel that same kind of impact in their lives.

Exciting Resources for Your Youth Ministry

At Risk: Bringing Hope to Hurting Teenagers

Dr. Scott Larson

Discover how to meet the needs of hurting teenagers with these practical suggestions, honest answers, and tools to help you evaluate your existing programs. Plus, you'll get real-life insights about what it takes to include kids others have left behind. If you believe the Gospel is for everyone, this book is for you! Includes a special introduction by Duffy Robbins and a foreword by Dean Borgman.

ISBN 0-7644-2091-7

All-Star Games From All-Star Youth Leaders

The ultimate game book—from the biggest names in youth ministry! All-time no-fail favorites from Wayne Rice, Les Christie, Rich Mullins, Tiger McLuen, Darrell Pearson, Dave Stone, Bart Campolo, Steve Fitzhugh, and 21 others! You get all the games you'll need for any situation. Plus, you get practical advice about how to design your own games and tricks for turning a *good* game into a *great* game!

ISBN 0-7644-2020-8

The Youth Worker's Encyclopedia of Bible-Teaching Ideas

Here are the most comprehensive idea books available for youth workers. With more than 365 creative ideas in each of these 400-page encyclopedias, there's at least one idea for every book of the Bible. You'll find ideas for retreats and overnighters…learning games…adventures…projects…affirmations…parties… prayers… music…devotions…skits…and more!

Old Testament   ISBN 1-55945-184-X
New Testament   ISBN 1-55945-183-1

Awesome Worship Services for Youth

These 12 complete worship services involve kids in 4 key elements of worship: celebration, reflection, symbolic action, and declaration of God's Truth. Flexible and dynamic services each last about an hour and will bring your group closer to God.

ISBN 0-7644-2057-7

More Resources for Your Youth Ministry

New Directions for Youth Ministry
Wayne Rice, Chap Clark and others

Discover ministry strategies and models that are working in *real* churches...with *real* kids. Readers get practical help evaluating what will work in their ministries and a candid look at the pros and cons of implementing each strategy.

ISBN 0-7644-2103-4

Hilarious Skits for Youth Ministry
Chris Chapman

Easy-to-act and fun-to-watch, these 8 youth group skits are guaranteed to get your kids laughing—and listening. These skits help your kids discover spiritual truths! They last from 5 to 15 minutes, so there's a skit to fit into any program!

ISBN 0-7644-2033-X

Character Counts!: 40 Youth Ministry Devotions
From Extraordinary Christians
Karl Leuthauser

Inspire your kids, introduce them to authentic heroes, and help them celebrate their heritage of faith with these 40 youth ministry devotions from the lives of extraordinary Christians. These brief, interactive devotions provide powerful testimonies from faithful Christians like Corrie ten Boom, Mother Teresa, Dietrich Bonhoeffer, and Harriet Tubman. Men and women who lived their faith without compromise, demonstrated Christlike character, and whose true stories inspire teenagers to do the same!

ISBN 0-7644-2075-5

On-the-Edge Games for Youth Ministry
Karl Rohnke

Author Karl Rohnke is a recognized, established game guru, and he's packed this book with quality, cooperative, communication-building, brain-stretching, crowdbreaking, flexible, can't-wait-to-try-them games youth leaders love. Readers can tie in these games to Bible-learning opportunities or just play them.

ISBN 0-7644-2058-5